Heroes for Young Readers

Written by Renee Taft Meloche
Illustrated by Bryan Pollard

Adoniram Judson
Amy Carmichael
Betty Greene
Cameron Townsend
Corrie ten Boom
David Livingstone
Eric Liddell
George Müller

Gladys Aylward
Hudson Taylor
Jim Elliot
Jonathan Goforth
Lottie Moon
Mary Slessor
Nate Saint
William Carey

Heroes of History for Young Readers

Written by Renee Taft Meloche
Illustrated by Bryan Pollard

Clara Barton
George Washington
George Washington Carver
Meriwether Lewis

…and more coming soon

*Heroes for Young Readers Activity Guides and audio CDs
are now available! See the back of this book for more information.*

For a free catalog of books and materials contact
YWAM Publishing, P.O. Box 55787, Seattle, WA 98155
1-800-922-2143, www.ywampublishing.com

HEROES OF HISTORY FOR YOUNG READERS

CLARA BARTON

Courage to Serve

Written by Renee Taft Meloche
Illustrated by Bryan Pollard

Emerald Books
P.O. BOX 635
LYNNWOOD, WA 98046

A girl named Clara Barton, born
    in eighteen twenty-one,
played war games with her father to
    pretend and have some fun.

They made up battle scenes by using
    peas for cavalry,
some tiny twigs for cannons, and
    corn seeds for infantry.

Her father—once a soldier—
    encouraged her to be
a person who would honor God
    and help people in need.

Young Clara lived in Massachusetts,
    where she loved to ride
the horses on her family's farm
    and climb tall trees outside.

Though shy, she went to boarding school,
    where she felt all alone.
She cried so hard and was so scared
    her father took her home.

One day, from high up on a roof,
        her brother David fell
and afterward had headaches and
        was just not getting well.

Though Clara was just ten years old,
        she soon became his nurse.
She fed him soup and soothed his brow
        and put her brother first.

A doctor gave her leeches, and
        he showed her how to get
these dark and slimy creatures to
        suck blood from David's neck.

Back then some doctors thought that having
        too much blood was bad,
so Clara bravely did the job
        despite the fears she had.

She nursed her brother for two years
        till he felt well and whole,
and helping him made her less timid
        and a bit more bold.

When Clara turned eighteen, her parents
thought she might explore
a teaching job to build up her
self-confidence some more.

So Clara started teaching school,
and on her first day found
that four tall teenage boys in class
just laughed and fooled around.

When lunchtime came, she thought and thought
    to come up with a way
to earn the boys' respect so that
    they'd study hard each day.

She saw the students playing with
    a baseball and a bat—
a sport she'd practiced as a child
    and now was quite good at.

Though Clara was just five feet tall,
    she stood up fearlessly.
"Hey, over here!" she yelled to them.
    "Just throw the ball to me."

A large boy threw it hard and fast.
　　She caught it with one hand.
"Just twist your wrist," she said and showed
　　them so they'd understand.
"Your pitch will be much faster." Then
　　she threw the spinning ball.
It sailed right past the catcher and
　　it hit an old stone wall.

The boys, impressed, invited her
　　to hit the ball and run.
She raced around from base to base;
　　they all had so much fun.

And things were very different in
　　the school that afternoon.
From then on all the boys worked hard
　　inside the small classroom.

Yes, Clara loved her job, and her
　　success in teaching grew,
but after she'd taught thirteen years,
　　she looked for something new.

So Clara traveled from the North
    to Washington, D.C.,
while all the states debated whether
    slaves should be set free.

Now Lincoln, who was president,
    said slavery was wrong,
but Southern states said that their way
    of life should go right on.

Though they were all Americans,
    they argued fiercely, and
in eighteen sixty-one the U.S.
    Civil War began.

One day some Union soldiers, from
    the North, arrived by train.
Attacked by Southerners, they all
    looked battered and in pain.

So Clara sprang to action, helping
    out the best she could.
She passed out bandages and blankets,
    food and other goods.

Not far off in Virginia,
    which was a Southern state,
the Union soldiers lost a fight;
    their need for aid was great.

The wounded came to Washington,
    and Clara helped them eat,
wrote letters to their loved ones, and
    put socks upon their feet.

Yet Clara knew that other men
    had died on battlefields
since no one had been there to help.
    So she made an appeal,
requesting that she go up to
    the front lines of the fight.
But she was told that for a woman
    this was just not right.

Persistent, Clara asked again.
    She said, "I have supplies,
like bandages and salves and clothes,
    to help save many lives."

At last one colonel said that she
    could go to the front lines
so she could rush life-saving care
    to wounded men on time.

So Clara went into Virginia,
    eager to provide
the help that she could offer with
    five wagons of supplies.

Arriving at the front lines, Clara
    sighed: the scene looked grim.
The men had cuts and broken bones,
    and some had lost a limb.

Men everywhere were moaning, and
    she shuddered at the sight
but gathered up her courage, and
    for two long days and nights
she cleaned men's wounds, encouraged them,
    and gave them clothes to wear.
She also helped the wounded of
    the Southern army there.

These soldiers—the Confederates—
    cried tears of gratitude.
They thanked her for her kindness and
    her helpful attitude.

Then two weeks later cannons boomed;
    more fighting had begun.
Immediately Clara packed
    and headed for Bull Run.

She pulled into the station there,
    arriving on a train.
She looked around and witnessed thousands,
    bloody, bruised, and maimed.

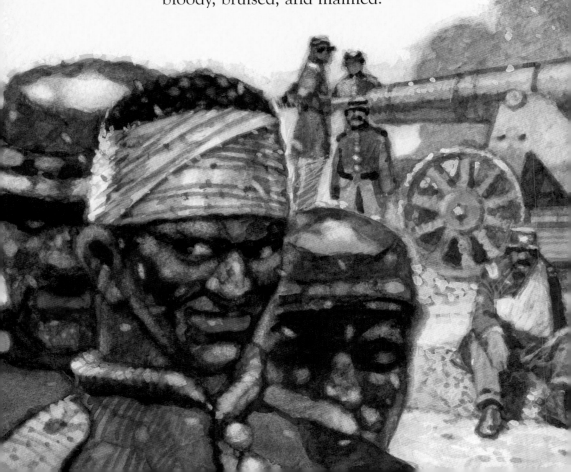

She quickly bandaged many wounds—
    for broken arms made slings.
She piled up straw to warm the men
    and ease their suffering.

She fed the men a mix of sugar,
    wine, and cracker crumbs.
"Do not give up," she gently whispered
    to them, one by one.

A few weeks later Clara went
    by wagon with a group
to Antietam, in Maryland,
    and nursed more wounded troops.

While there she gave one man a drink,
    and as she held his head,
a bullet barely missed her, and
    it hit the man instead.

She could not save this soldier, but
    she said a heartfelt prayer,
then dashed from one man to another,
    giving each man care.

At nightfall Clara heard a doctor
    say he had no light.
"Five hundred men will die because
    I cannot work tonight."

She led him from the small house he
    was using on a farm
and showed him all the lanterns that
    now lit up one big barn.

"I brought these lamps," said Clara, "so
    your work can still go on."
The doctor, thankful, would no longer
    have to wait till dawn.

The war went on, and Clara worked
    so hard that she was called
the "Angel of the Battlefield"
    by doctors, troops, and all.

The Union finally won the war
    in eighteen sixty-five.
In four years Clara's work had saved
    a great, great many lives.

And afterward she shared her nursing
    stories round the States,
until she moved to Switzerland
    to take a restful break.

While there a doctor told her of
    a great organization
that cared for soldiers on both sides
    of any confrontation.

"This Red Cross has been joined," he said,
    "by over thirty nations,
but not yet by America,
    a very great frustration."

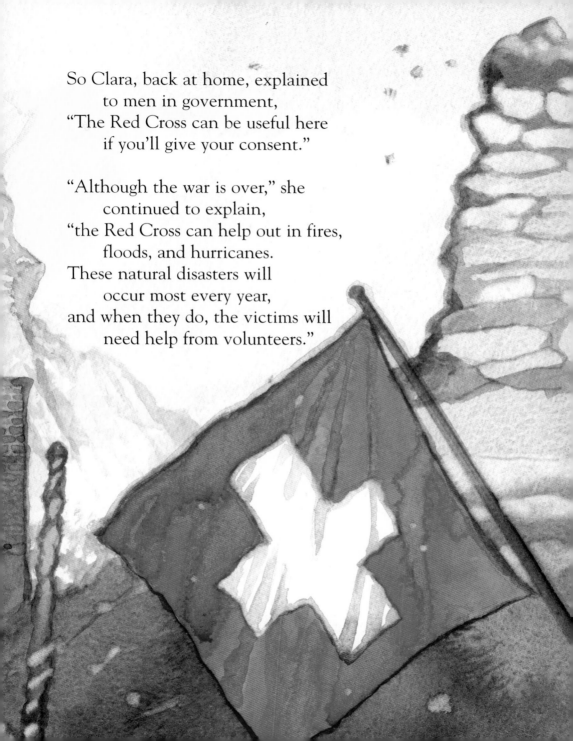

So Clara, back at home, explained
to men in government,
"The Red Cross can be useful here
if you'll give your consent."

"Although the war is over," she
continued to explain,
"the Red Cross can help out in fires,
floods, and hurricanes.
These natural disasters will
occur most every year,
and when they do, the victims will
need help from volunteers."

America soon joined with other
        nations and agreed
to follow Red Cross principles,
        with Clara taking lead.

When forest fires raged across
        a part of the Midwest,
the Red Cross gave out clothes and food
        to all those in distress.

A steamboat for the Red Cross helped
        deliver many goods
when floods hit Indiana and
        Ohio. Lots of wood
was brought so that new shelters could
        be built on higher ground.
And as the steamboat traveled down
        the river, Clara found
the sights to be as awful as
        some battlegrounds she'd seen,
for dogs and houses floated past
        and helpless people screamed.

The steamboat's symbol was a cross
        that had been painted red,
and soon reports about the Red
        Cross and its mission spread.

In eighteen ninety-three a sudden
        new disaster came:
a Carolina island was
        hit by a hurricane.

Though Clara now was aging, she
        could not ignore the needs
of homeless, starving people whom
        she had to house and feed.

She taught the people how to grow
        crops edible and sweet,
not cotton like before, but fresh-grown
        foods that they could eat.

Some women had donated gowns,
        so Clara found a way
to sew the fancy cloth into
        good clothes for work and play.

The Red Cross workers also helped
        build thousands of new homes,
so people who had suffered loss
        could manage on their own.

When Clara Barton finally
    retired at eighty-three,
she rested from her many years of
    service happily.

She'd overcome her shyness to
    help soldiers during war
and victims of disasters, who
    were homeless, hungry, poor.

Her courage and compassion still
    impact the world today,
as Red Cross workers serve the needy
    near and far away.

Christian Heroes: Then & Now

by Janet and Geoff Benge

Adoniram Judson: Bound for Burma
Amy Carmichael: Rescuer of Precious Gems
Betty Greene: Wings to Serve
Brother Andrew: God's Secret Agent
Cameron Townsend: Good News in Every Language
Clarence Jones: Mr. Radio
Corrie ten Boom: Keeper of the Angels' Den
Count Zinzendorf: Firstfruit
C. S. Lewis: Man, Myth, and Imagination
C. T. Studd: No Retreat
David Livingstone: Africa's Trailblazer
Eric Liddell: Something Greater Than Gold
Florence Young: Mission Accomplished
George Müller: The Guardian of Bristol's Orphans
Gladys Aylward: The Adventure of a Lifetime
Hudson Taylor: Deep in the Heart of China
Ida Scudder: Healing Bodies, Touching Hearts
Jim Elliot: One Great Purpose
John Wesley: The World as His Parish
John Williams: Messenger of Peace
Jonathan Goforth: An Open Door in China
Lillian Trasher: The Greatest Wonder in Egypt
Loren Cunningham: Into All the World
Lottie Moon: Giving Her All for China
Mary Slessor: Forward into Calabar
Nate Saint: On a Wing and a Prayer
Rachel Saint: A Star in the Jungle
Rowland Bingham: Into Africa's Interior
Sundar Singh: Footprints Over the Mountains
Wilfred Grenfell: Fisher of Men
William Booth: Soup, Soap, and Salvation
William Carey: Obliged to Go

Heroes for Young Readers and Heroes of History for Young Readers are based on the Christian Heroes: Then & Now and Heroes of History biographies by Janet and Geoff Benge. Don't miss out on these exciting, true adventures for ages ten and up!

Continued on the next page...

Heroes of History
by Janet and Geoff Benge

Abraham Lincoln: A New Birth of Freedom
Benjamin Franklin: Live Wire
Christopher Columbus: Across the Ocean Sea
Clara Barton: Courage under Fire
Daniel Boone: Frontiersman
Douglas MacArthur: What Greater Honor
George Washington Carver: From Slave to Scientist
George Washington: True Patriot
Harriet Tubman: Freedombound
John Adams: Independence Forever
John Smith: A Foothold in the New World
Laura Ingalls Wilder: A Storybook Life
Meriwether Lewis: Off the Edge of the Map
Orville Wright: The Flyer
Theodore Roosevelt: An American Original
Thomas Edison: The Inventor
William Penn: Liberty and Justice for All

...and more coming soon. Unit study curriculum guides are also available.

Heroes for Young Readers Activity Guides
Educational and Character-Building Lessons for Children
by Renee Taft Meloche

Heroes for Young Readers Activity Guide for Books 1–4
Gladys Aylward, Eric Liddell, Nate Saint, George Müller

Heroes for Young Readers Activity Guide for Books 5–8
Amy Carmichael, Corrie ten Boom, Mary Slessor, William Carey

Heroes for Young Readers Activity Guide for Books 9–12
Betty Greene, David Livingstone, Adoniram Judson, Hudson Taylor

Heroes for Young Readers Activity Guide for Books 13–16
Jim Elliot, Cameron Townsend, Jonathan Goforth, Lottie Moon

...and more coming soon.

Designed to accompany the vibrant Heroes for Young Readers books, these fun-filled activity guides lead young children through a variety of character-building and educational activities. Pick and choose from the activities or follow the included thirteen-week syllabus. An audio CD with book readings, songs, and fun activity tracks is available for each Activity Guide.

For a free catalog of books and materials contact
YWAM Publishing, P.O. Box 55787, Seattle, WA 98155
1-800-922-2143, www.ywampublishing.com